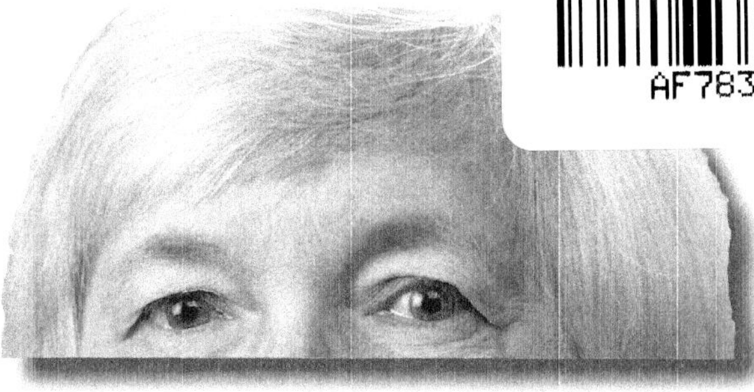

JANET YELLEN

FEDERAL RESERVE CHAIR

MARIE A. BUSSING

ANAPHORA LITERARY PRESS

AUGUSTA, GEORGIA

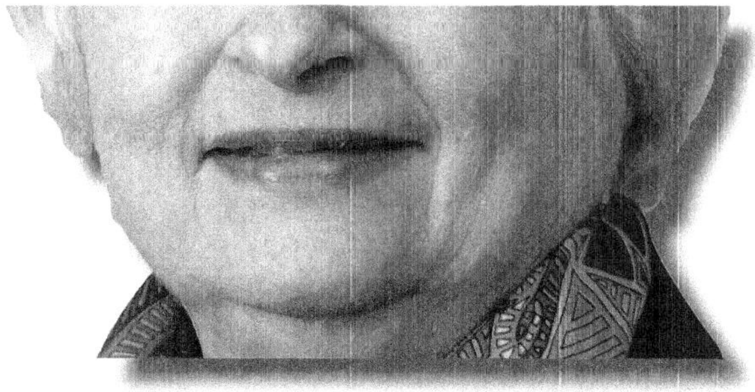

Anaphora Literary Press
2419 Southdale Drive
Hephzibah, GA 30815
http://anaphoraliterary.com

Book design by Anna Faktorovich, Ph.D.

Edited by: Christina Wordham

Published in 2015 by Anaphora Literary Press

Janet Yellen: Federal Reserve Chair
Marie A. Bussing—1st edition.

Anaphora

Print ISBN-13: 978-1-68114-203-6
ISBN-10: 1-681142-03-1
EBook ISBN-13: 978-1-68114-204-3
ISBN-10: 1-681142-04-X

Library of Congress Control Number: 2015915329

JANET YELLEN

FEDERAL RESERVE CHAIR

MARIE A. BUSSING

CONTENTS

This book is dedicated to JKR
For love, dedication, and encouragement.

"I am absolutely confident that she will be an exceptional Chair of the Federal Reserve. I should add that she'll be the first woman to lead the Fed in its 100-year history."

–President Obama's nomination of Dr. Janet Yellen as Chair of the Board of Governors of the Federal Reserve System, October 9, 2013

Introduction

The Chair of the Federal Reserve System is one of the most powerful jobs in the world. Why? The Federal Reserve, or "Fed" for short, is the central bank of the United States. The Fed is a governmental agency in charge of the nation's monetary and financial system. The U.S. has the largest economic system of any nation in the world, at near $18 trillion.

Fig. 1. Ben Bernanke, Former Chairman of the Federal Reserve Board of Governors, at a House Financial Services Committee

The Federal Reserve System consists of a Board of Governors in Washington, DC, the Federal Open Market Committee, 12 regional Federal Reserve District Banks, plus 25 bank branches.

The Fed is responsible for:

- conducting the nation's monetary policy by influencing

money and credit conditions in the economy,
- supervising and regulating banks and other important financial institutions,
- maintaining the stability of the financial system, and
- providing certain financial services to the government and financial institutions.

There are seven members that make up the Board of Governors. These members are typically economists, lawyers, or individuals with governmental or banking regulatory experience. Each member is appointed by the President of the U.S. and confirmed by the Senate for a 14-year term of office. The President additionally chooses, and the Senate confirms, two members of the Board to be Chairman and Vice Chairman, each with a four-year term. The responsibilities of the Board of Governors are extensive, and the board has a great deal of control over the entire U.S. economy, the macroeconomy, because the Fed is the monetary authority for the U.S.

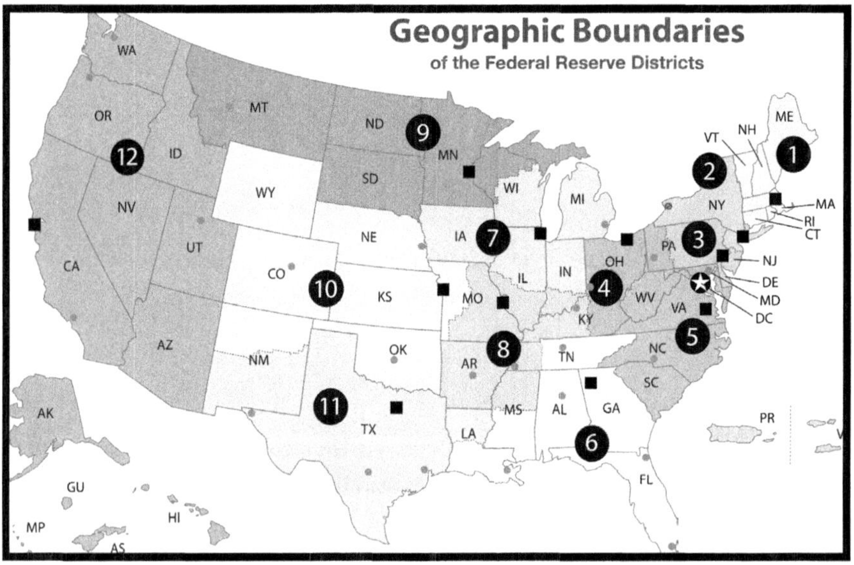

Fig. 2. Map of the Twelve Federal Reserve Districts

The seven board members also sit on the 12-member Federal Open Market Committee (known as the FOMC). This group consists of the Board of Governors, plus five other members chosen from among the District Bank presidents. The group meets every six to eight weeks and has sole responsibility for making decisions on credit conditions in the U.S. economy. This group is sometimes informally known as the Interest Rate Committee, because influencing interest rates by controlling the amount of money in the economy is their job. Although monetary policy is extremely complex, the basic concept is that when there is more money in the economy, the easier it is to get a loan, and interest rates are low. When less money is available in the economy, credit is tighter, it is harder to get a loan, and interest rates rise.

The Chair of the Board of Governors always holds the Chair position with the FOMC. The Vice Chair of the FOMC is always the president of the Federal Reserve Bank of New York, and the other District Bank presidents rotate into the four remaining seats on the FOMC. The reason New York is always the Vice Chair is because New York has the trading desk for the Fed, meaning that all of the buying and selling of bonds to influence credit conditions goes through the New York Fed.

Janet Yellen began her 14-year term at the Fed in 2010, serving as Vice Chair until 2014. Through Yellen's strong work in guiding the economy as the Vice Chair, and her known leadership as a consensus builder, Yellen was one of just a few considered to guide the Central Bank. Yellen was nominated by President Barack Obama for the lead position, confirmed by the Senate, and took office on February 1, 2014. Let's examine her journey to becoming the top money manager.

Fig. 3. President Barack Obama at Yellen's Nomination

The Federal Reserve dates to 1913, organized in response to the severe banking panic of 1907, and accompanying weak financial system. On December 23, 1913, what U.S. president signed the Federal Reserve Act into law?

a. Barack Obama
b. Bill Clinton
c. Franklin Delano Roosevelt
d. Woodrow Wilson

Answer: d. Woodrow Wilson, whose presidential term was from March 4, 1913–March 4, 1921.

Fig. 4. The First Federal Reserve Signing with Woodrow Wilson

Chapter 1

Early Life and Education

Janet Louise Yellen was born on August 13, 1946, in Brooklyn, New York, to an educated family. Her mother, Anna Blumenthal Yellen, was an elementary school teacher, and her father, Julius Yellen, a family doctor. Anna left teaching to raise Janet and her older brother, John, who is now Program Director for Archaeology at the National Science Foundation.

Yellen was always a keen academic. In 1963, she graduated from Fort Hamilton High School in Brooklyn as valedictorian of her class and the class scholar. Busy in high school, she was editor-in-chief of the school newspaper, *The Pilot*. She was also a member of the honor society, the boosters club, the history club, and the psychology club.

Yellen went on to study at Pembroke College in Brown University, Providence, RI. While there, Yellen tried her hand at the newspaper business, joining the Business Board of *The Brown Daily Herald* during her freshman year. Although successful at newspaper writing, economics was Yellen's calling, and her early economics writings were described as brilliant. She graduated summa cum laude from Brown University in 1967 with a B.A. degree in economics and continued on to earn her Ph.D. in economics from Yale University in 1971, where she was privileged to study under Nobel Prize-winning (1981) Keynesian economist James Tobin (1918–2002) . Tobin was a macroeconomist who believed in government intervention to stabilize the economy. It was Tobin who incited her interest in economics, serving as not only her academic adviser, but lifelong mentor.

Economics teachers are important at the grade school, middle school, high school and college level. Those teaching about economics could cover a wide variety of economic, monetary and financial subjects. After all, economics is a social science studying how individuals, businesses, governments and nations make choices based on allocating scarce resources in order to satisfy their unlimited wants. College courses are often divided into two semesters: macroeconomics, which is the study of the whole economy, and covers unemployment, inflation and output; and microeconomics, which concentrates on the behavior of individual consumers and markets.

What types of topics might you find in an economics course?

a. Supply and demand analysis
b. Profit and competition
c. Unemployment and inflation
d. All of the above

Answer: d. All of the above are among a wide variety of topics covered in an economics course.

Fig. 5. Treasury Secretary Jack Lew and Federal Reserve Chair Janet Yellen, February 5, 2014

Chapter 2

Family Life

After completing her Ph.D. in 1971, Yellen taught economics at Harvard University. From 1977 to 1979, Yellen served as an economist with the Federal Reserve's Board of Governors. At lunch at the Federal Reserve cafeteria she became acquainted with George Akerlof, an economist and University of California, Berkeley professor, who was on a temporary assignment at the Federal Reserve in Washington DC.

Yellen and Akerlof were quickly smitten, because not only were they compatible on a personal level, but they agreed and liked to discuss economics as well.

Within less than a year of meeting, the two were married. Both taught at London School of Economics and Political Science from 1978 to 1980. When the couple returned to the U.S., Yellen joined the faculty of the University of California, Berkeley. Yellen has written many economic papers, including some co-authored with her husband, Akerlof, who in 2001, won the Nobel Prize in Economics Sciences.

Yellen and Akerlof are a strong economic duo, working individually on a wide variety of macroeconomic issues, but also collaborating on research. Both have long been concerned with the causes of unemployment—the circumstances that cause people to lose their jobs and not have opportunities to find new work.

While both have had challenging jobs, they still devoted much of their time and energy to raising their son, Robert, who was born in 1981. Today, Robert is also in the family business. He is an economist in the Department of Economics at the University of Warwick, UK. The Akerlof family has a nice life, traveling extensively and enjoying hobbies such as collecting stamps.

Fig. 5. George A. Akerlof, Nobel economics Laureate and Yellen's Husband, at Berkeley

Fig. 6. Nobelist, George Akerlof, discussing economics during a television interview

Who is George Akerlof? George A. Akerlof was born on June 17, 1940, in New Haven, Connecticut. He received his BA degree from Yale in 1962 and his Ph.D. degree from MIT in 1966. He taught economics at the University of California, Berkeley from 1966 to 2010. Akerlof was a visiting scholar with the International Monetary Fund from 2010 to 2014.

In 2001 Akerlof won the Nobel Prize for Economics (shared with Michael Spence and Joseph Stiglitz) for laying the foundation for the theory of markets with asymmetric information. He noted certain markets have asymmetric information, meaning one side has more information than the other side. An example might be how the borrower of a bank loan has more information than the loan officer on the likelihood that he or she will repay the loan. The loan officers will attempt to compensate for the asymmetric information by checking credit scores, asking for guarantees on the loan, and investigating past income statements and tax returns.

The Federal Reserve Sets a Record for 2014!

The Federal Reserve made a record profit in 2014, mainly from interest on the bonds it owns. Guess how much?

a. $98.7 billion
b. $10
c. $5.2 million
d. $27,000

Answer: a. $98.7 billion. The Fed turned over a record breaking $98.7 billion in profits to the U.S. Treasury in 2014. After paying its expenses, the Fed turns the remainder over to the Treasury.

Chapter 3

Academic and Professional Career

After two years teaching in London, in 1980 Akerlof returned to the faculty of the University of California, Berkeley, and Yellen also joined the faculty there as a professor. Then in 1994, Yellen took a leave for governmental and political opportunities. She served for three years as a member of the Federal Reserve Board of Governors, where she argued for transparency and a more open Federal Reserve. Yellen wanted the Fed to ramp up its communication with the public, and promoted holding more press conferences and publicly discussing economic goals for the U.S. economy.

Yellen's journey then took her to become Chair of the White House Council of Economic Advisers from 1997 to 1999. She was appointed to the position by U.S. President Bill Clinton, and during that same time period she also chaired the Economic Policy Committee of the Organization for Economic Cooperation and Development. Yellen resigned the appointment for family reasons and to return to her teaching position at Berkeley. Today, Yellen is Professor Emeritus (a title given to a retired professor who may retain the title for life) at the University of California, Berkeley, where she was the Eugene E. and Catherine M. Trefethen Professor of Business and Professor of Economics.

Fig. 7. The Facade of the Old Federal Reserve Bank of San Francisco at 400 Sansome Street

A few years after her return to Berkeley, the Fed was calling and Yellen soon returned. She served as President and Chief Executive Officer of the Federal Reserve Bank of San Francisco from 2004 to 2010. San Francisco is the 12th district and the largest, covering approximately 1.3 million square miles. This is roughly 35 percent of the area of the U.S. The San Francisco District is expansive and includes nine states—Alaska, Arizona, California, Hawaii, Idaho, Nevada, Oregon, Utah, and Washington—plus American Samoa, Guam, and the Commonwealth of the Northern Mariana Islands. Yellen was well-regarded as the head of the San Francisco Fed bank. She is known to be a methodical thinker because she does not make decisions quickly, rather taking her time to think through the issues thoroughly. She is known also for her foresight, making early warnings about the faltering real estate market and its potential negative impact on the economy prior to the 2008 crash in real estate prices.

Yellen's reputation was strong and on April 28, 2010, President Obama nominated Yellen to serve as Vice Chair of the Federal Reserve. Confirmed by the Senate, on October 4, 2010, Yellen was sworn in for a four-year term ending October 4, 2014. Yellen simultaneously began her 14-year term as a member of the Federal Reserve Board of Governors which expires on January 31, 2024.

Federal Reserve notes (a.k.a. dollars) are designed and printed by which agency?

a. The Bureau of Engraving and Printing
b. The U.S. Mint
c. The Federal Reserve
d. The Environmental Protection Agency

Answer: a. The Bureau of Engraving and Printing has two production facilities, in Washington, DC, and Fort Worth, Texas.

Money Supply and Interest Rates

The Federal Reserve is in charge of money supply in the United States. The amount of money in the country greatly affects the interest rate for borrowing and for saving.

If the Fed expands money supply, how does this affect the overall level of interest?

a. Expands
b. Falls
c. Stays the Same

Answer: b. Falls. As money is expanded, interest rates will fall. The more money in the economy the easier it is to get a loan, there is less competition for funds, and interest rates will decrease.

Chapter 4

Federal Reserve Top Position

Ben Bernanke, 14th Chair of the Federal Reserve, served two terms as the Federal Reserve Chair. He was nominated by Republican President George W. Bush in 2006, and re-nominated in 2010 by Democratic President Barack Obama. In June 2013, President Obama hinted that Bernanke was not interested in returning for another term, and then the speculation began. Bernanke, a well-known depression scholar and Princeton economist, received accolades as Fed Chair. This chair presided over the tough 2007–2009 Great Recession, pumping large sums of money into the economy in order to provide a boost. Bernanke is known for the Fed's easy money policies and low interest rates designed to encourage borrowing and spending to stimulate the economy. Also known for transparency and clear communication at the Fed, meaning the board must be accountable to the public for their decisions, Bernanke largely received an "A" during his tenure, and would be a tough act to follow.

Who was going to be the 15th Fed Chair? With the internet, television, social and print media closely monitoring the actions and decisions of those in strong political and economic positions, the head of the Fed is not only the country's top economist, keeping inflation low and employment strong, but represents the Central Bank. The Fed Chair testifies twice a year before Congress with the Semiannual Monetary Policy Report to Congress about the progress of the economy and the direction of monetary policy, testifies before Congress on numerous other issues and meets periodically with the secretary of the Treasury, as well as holds press conferences to the public.

All eyes are on the Fed because unemployment and inflation affects all Americans. People feel the pain when unemployment is high and they have lost their jobs, unable to find worthwhile employment. People are affected by unemployment in numerous ways other than their pocketbooks. Depression, trouble at home, broken friendships, and depletion of skills are all costs of unemployment.

Inflation, a sustained increase in prices, is troublesome to people, too. Americans want to know what the Fed is doing to keep inflation low. As prices rise, consumers are unable to keep up their standard of living with no corresponding rise in income. Inflation causes people to spend more now, because they anticipate prices will continue to go up, causing an inflation spiral. The purchasing power of your savings account and investments is depleted.

The list of potential candidates to head the Fed in 2014 was short—Larry Summers, a former economic policy adviser for Obama; Donald L. Kohn, Fed Vice Chair from 2006 to 2010; and Janet Yellen, current Fed Vice Chair, a well-received and proven commodity. Not only is it important for the public to have a Fed Chair that they feel comfortable with, it is important that the other Board of Governors and the FOMC members enjoy working with the Fed Chair, as well.

The Board of Governors work in Washington, DC full time. They are in charge of banking regulation and two monetary policy tools—reserve requirements (the percentage of checkable deposits that banks must keep on hand), and the discount rate (interest rate at which banks may borrow money from the Fed), along with other financial issues. These are all important because we need sound financial institutions, banks need to keep some money on hand for issues such as withdrawals, and it is necessary to maintain a reasonable rate for banks to borrow money in times of need or emergency. Another consideration is appointing a Chair who can build an educated consensus. Remember that the FOMC is composed of all seven Board of Governors, plus five of the 12 Federal Reserve Bank presidents (bank presidents rotate membership, except NY which is always on the board). The Fed Chair leads the FOMC discussions and plans the meeting agenda, but each of the 12 members has an equal vote. In other words, members do not have to vote with the Chair and occasionally do not.

The FOMC sets monetary policy on the buying and selling of bonds, which influences interest rates, specifically the Federal Funds rate. The Federal Funds rate (also called the interbank borrowing rate) is the rate at which banks may borrow money from one another. Ben Bernanke had set the Fed policy on interest rates to historically low levels, so businesses and consumers could borrow more easily to build buildings, buy homes, and start businesses, which in turn would stimulate the economy. There is a large amount of money, a.k.a liquidity, in the market. The new chairman would need to build a consensus to decide if this is the appropriate path to stay on, or is it time to tighten money and raise rates. An increase in interest rates tends to suggest a strengthening economy. Higher interest rates mean more is earned on investment accounts. It could potentially increase household income, and be a boom for the economy, increasing jobs and spending. These are all tough decisions.

Yellen is a known consensus builder, knows her economics, and is a deep thinker. She did a good job as Vice Chair. In October 2013, President Barack Obama nominated Yellen as Chair of the Federal Reserve. Yellen, a Democrat, is the first woman to head the Central Bank.

At the November 13, 2013 confirmation hearing, Yellen stated, "In the past two decades, and especially under Chairman Bernanke, the Federal Reserve has provided more and clearer information about its goals....I have strongly supported this commitment to openness and transparency, and will continue to do so if I am confirmed and serve as Chair." On January 6, 2014, the Senate voted 56–26 to approve Yellen as Chair of the Fed, with her start date set for February 1. In November 2014, Akerlof, joined Yellen in in DC and accepted a position as University Professor at Georgetown.

What is the salary for the top Federal Reserve officials?

Congress sets the salaries of the Board of Governors. For 2015, the Chairman earns an annual salary of $199,700. The annual salary of the other board members is $179,700.

Fig. 8. Vice Chair of the Federal Reserve and former Governor of the Bank of Israel, Stanley Fischer

Who is the current Vice Chair of the Federal Reserve? This individual took office as a member of the Board of Governors of the Federal on May 28, 2014.

a. Barack Obama
b. John Boehner
c. John Kerry
d. Stanley Fischer

Answer: d. Stanley Fischer. Prior to his appointment to the Board, Dr. Fischer was governor of the Bank of Israel from 2005 through 2013. Fischer received his bachelor's and master's degrees in economics from the London School of Economics, and his Ph.D. in economics from the MIT. Fischer also served as the first deputy managing director of the International Monetary Fund and chief economist of the World Bank.

How long is the term for the Chairman and Vice Chairman of the Federal Reserve?

a. One year
b. Two years
c. Three years
d. Four years

Answer: d. Four years. The Chairman and Vice Chairman of the Board serve four year terms, and they may be reappointed to those roles and serve until their 14 year terms as Board members expire.

Chapter 5

Awards and Appointments

Awards are significant recognitions. They not only encourage the recipient and others to strive harder, but awards validate hard work. They make parents, friends, children, spouses and other family members proud. You know how proud your parents are of you when you get an award at school. Awards recognize excellence, effort, and ability, and Yellen has shown that she is a hard worker, always striving for excellence.

Yellen has received numerous accolades for her contributions to the field of economics. She served as a Guggenheim Fellow (for those who have demonstrated exceptional capacity for productive scholarship or exceptional creative ability in the arts) in 1986 in Social Science, and received the Wilbur Lucius Cross Medal (an honor presented each year by the Graduate School Alumni Association) from Yale University in 1997.

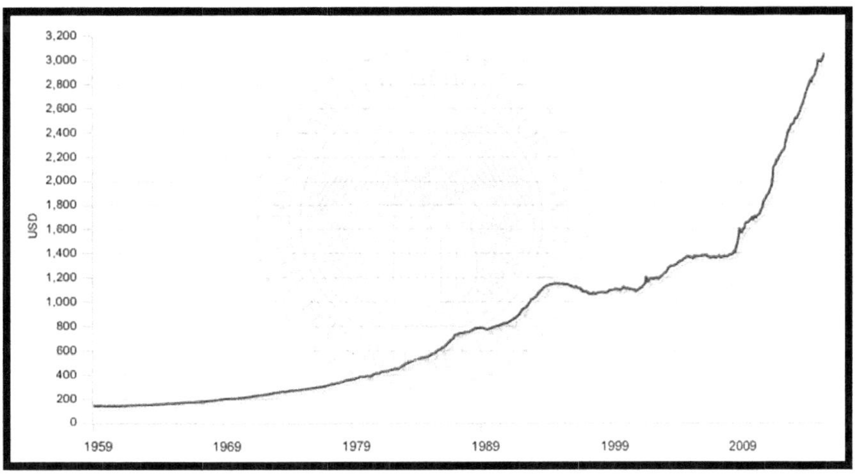

Fig. 9. Historical Monthly and Seasonally Adjusted M1 USD, in Billions, FederalReserve.gov

An honorary doctorate is the highest level of academic recognition bestowed by a university, but does not require academic work. Yellen received an honorary Doctor of Laws degree from Brown University in 1998, and an honorary Doctor of Humane Letters from Bard College in 2000.

Equally important to awards and recognitions for work are appointments and memberships. The organizations with which you associate reflect your interests. Yellen is a member of both the Council on Foreign Relations (headquartered in New York City, an independent, nonpartisan membership organization, think tank in U.S. foreign policy and international affairs) and the American Academy of Arts and Sciences (headquartered in Cambridge, Mass., a learned society and independent policy research center). She has served as President of the Western Economic Association International, Vice President of the American Economic Association and a Fellow of the Yale Corporation, the governing board and policy-making body for Yale University. Yellen's participation with such esteemed associations shows she values economics and education.

Fig. 10. US Currency

American Economic Association

The American Economic Association (AEA) was organized in 1885 at a meeting in Saratoga, New York, by a small group of people interested in economics. In 1923, it was incorporated in Washington, DC. There are currently approximately 18,000 members.

The purposes of the Association are:

1. The encouragement of economic research, especially the historical and statistical study of the actual conditions of industrial life.
2. The issue of publications on economic subjects.
3. The encouragement of perfect freedom of economic discussion. The Association as such will take no partisan attitude, nor will it commit its members to any position on practical economic questions.

Source: American Economic Association. www.aeweb.org.

Western Economic Association International

The Western Economic Association International (WEAI) was founded in 1922. Headquartered in Fountain Valley, California, WEAI is a non-profit educational organization. The WEAI has almost 1,800 members from across the globe, dedicated to encouraging and communicating economic research and analysis. The WEAI publishes two quarterly journals, *Economic Inquiry*, and *Contemporary Economic Policy*, along with hosting conferences and forums for economic research.

Source: Western Economic Association, www.weai.org.

It is important for the Federal Reserve Chair to understand all about money, because money greatly impacts the economy. How much do you think the U.S. has in checks, currency and travelers checks?

a. $99 million
b. $1.8 billion
c. $34 billion
d. $3.0 trillion

Answer: d. $3.0 trillion. This amount is referred to as M1 money supply, the lowest level of money, which is highly liquid and can be spent quickly. To picture how much money there is in the American economy, imagine $3 with twelve zeros following, or $3,000,000,000,000.

Source: Board of Governors, Money Stock Measures, H.6 release, August 6, 2015.

Chapter 6

Guiding the Country

Yellen, as new Chair of the Fed, said she planned to support the policies adopted under her predecessor, Ben Bernanke. This is true and she has held many news conferences, supporting the transparency that Bernanke had established.

Fig. 11. Yellen Sworn in by Fed Chairman Ben Bernanke in October 2010

She is interested in increasing employment in the U.S. In economics, this is referred to as being a dove on monetary policy.

When a person is a dove, they are more concerned about high unemployment than they are about an increase of inflation. They support monetary policies that involve keeping interest rates low, noting the detrimental effects from inflation will be small. The term "dove" comes from the calm nature of the bird, while the opposite nickname is a "hawk."

A hawk (a.k.a an inflation hawk) is generally concerned with inflation. They favor higher interest rates in order to keep inflation tame. Hawks maintain that higher interest rates will control spending, and thus bring down inflation and decrease recessionary possibilities. When growth rates are too high in the economy, hawks get concerned that inflation may run out of control.

What does this mean? Yellen is not overly concerned about the economy getting out of control and not inclined to tighten policy early in her term. She clearly cares about people having jobs, and Americans appreciate that caring quality from the economist. In a February 11, 2013 unemployment issues speech when she was Vice Chair, Yellen noted, "These are not just statistics to me. We know that long-term unemployment is devastating to workers and their families."

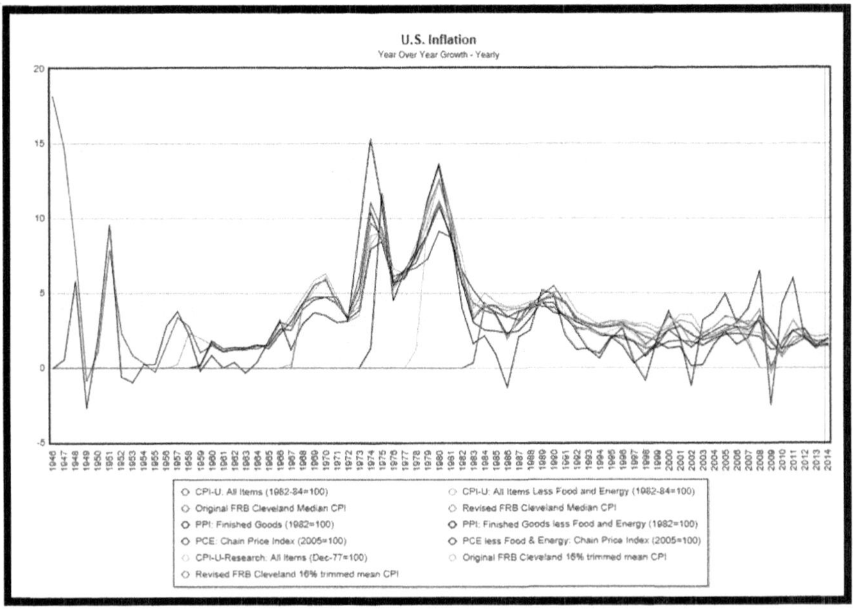

Fig. 12. Historical Annual U.S. Inflation Rate

In October 2014, the Federal Reserve with Yellen at the helm, ended the Fed's bond buying program, which was designed to provide liquidity and lower borrowing cost for people and businesses. This action is a sign that the Fed Chief sees strength in the American economy. It is also an indication that Yellen is a person of courage, who will do what she thinks is best for the economy, as not all investors saw the discontinuation of this program as a favorable action. The challenge for Yellen in 2015, deciding if and when to raise interest rates. Yellen has indicated she will not make a move until the economy is strong and is ready for upward tightening on rates. All signs point to Yellen as a cautious Fed Chair.

Yellen will be the person directing the course of the Federal Reserve to help with future unemployment and inflation issues in the U.S. People are going to keep watching Yellen and listening to what she says about the economy in the days ahead. Why? Because Janet Yellen is the face of the Fed.

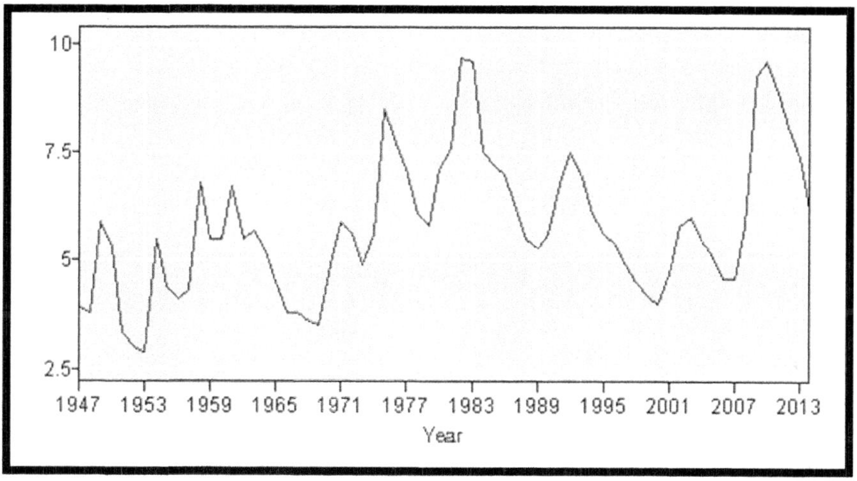

Fig. 13. Historical Annual U.S. Unemployment Rate; Source: Bureau of Labor Statistics

The Federal Reserve has its own unique measures of money. A broader measure of money is M2, an important classification of money because many people and businesses utilize this medium of exchange to make payments or hold as savings. M2 includes everything in M1 (currency, checks, and travelers checks) plus savings deposits, small time deposits, and money market mutual funds. It is vital for the Fed to keep track of money supply because the level of money affects interest rates and in the long-term, inflation. How much M2 money supply currently exists in the United States?

a. $12 trillion
b. $12 million
c. $12 billion
d. $12 quadrillion

Answer: a. $12 trillion. Yes, the U.S. economy has a total of $12,000,000,000,000 in M2!

Source: Board of Governors, Money Stock Measures, H.6 release, August 6, 2015.

Websites for the Junior Economist:

http://www.usmint.gov/kids/ The U.S. Mint's educational site for children is hours of fun. Trivia, games, mint history, coin collections, all make learning about money fun. Visit major moments in history with the H.I.P. Pocket Change Time Machine. When you leave this website you will be a coin historian!

https://www.federalreserveeducation.org/about-the-fed/history/ Click on for a discovery of the monetary system of the U.S. dating from the American Revolution to current times. If you are a history buff, here is your site.

https://philadelphiafed.org/education/federal-reserve-and-you/ The Federal Reserve Bank of Philadelphia has a fantastic video series. Watch video series *Federal Reserve and You, History of Central Banking in the United States, Money and Banking 101,* and many more.

http://www.stlouisfed.org/education_resources/glossary/ For an expansive economics and personal financial glossary, visit the St. Louis Fed website. Great dictionary. A link will allow you to make flash cards.

www.federalreserve.gov The Board of Governors of the Federal Reserve System. Click on About the Fed and you will see photos and bios of Chair Janet Yellen, along with all the other members of the Board. Explore Vice Chair Stanley Fisher's excellent resume, former chief economist of the World Bank, plus other outstanding board members.

https://kids.usa.gov/index.shtml Click on Money for Kids K–5 or 6–8 and open up a world of videos and exercises all related to money. You can even see how money is created in the Money Factory video.

Fig. 14. Janet Yellen's Official Federal Reserve Portrait

Appendix 1

Chronology

1946	Janet Louise Yellen was born on August 13, 1946, in Brooklyn, NY.
1963	Yellen graduates as valedictorian of Fort Hamilton High School in Brooklyn.
1967	Yellen graduates summa cum laude with a degree in economics from Brown University.
1971	Yellen graduates with a doctorate in economics from Yale University.
1978	Yellen marries economist George Akerlof.
1980	Yellen joins faculty at University of California, Berkeley.
1981	Yellen and Akerlof have a son, Robert.
1994-97	Yellen serves on Federal Reserve Board of Governors.
1997-99	Yellen serves as Chair of the White House Council of Economic Advisers.
1997-99	Yellen serves as Chair of the Economic Policy Committee of the Organization for Economic Cooperation and Development.
2010	Yellen begins four-year term as Vice Chair of the Federal Reserve.
2014	Yellen begins four-year term as Chair of the Federal Reserve. The Federal Reserve Board ended its bond buying program in October 2014.
2015	Yellen indicates she will not raise interest rates until the economy is strong.

Appendix 2

Female Heads

Janet Yellen may be the first women to head the Federal Reserve but she is not the only female head at a monetary authority. According to CentralBankNews.info, as of January 19, 2015, 16 out of 190 central banks were headed by a female chief, either on a full-time or interim basis. Women increasingly are rising to the top of the key monetary institutions as the head central banker. Although these institutions cover the globe, a central bank has many similarities such as guiding interest rates, managing money supply, regulating commercial banks, and acting as a government bank.

Following is a listing of the central banks headed by women and a quick peek into the backgrounds of these female chiefs.

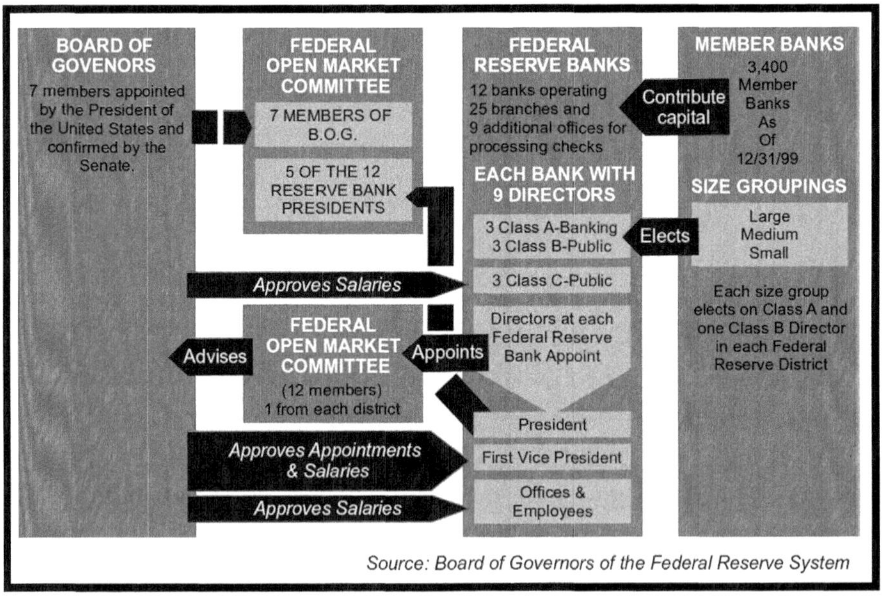

Fig. 15. Organization of the Federal Reserve System

Central Bank of Aruba

Jeanette R. Semeleer obtained undergraduate and master's degrees from the University of Toledo. She has led the central bank since 2008, holding the title of President, joining the central banks' Executive Committee in 2000. She heads the central bank of an island country covering 70 square miles, Aruba, located in the Southern Carribean. Tourism accounts for over 80 percent of the economy.

Central Bank of the Bahamas

Wendy Craigg obtained an undergraduate degree in economics and business from the College of Mount Saint Vincent, New York and a master's degree in economics from Fordham University. She was appointed Governor and Chairman of the Board of Directors in 2005, serving as Deputy Governor Deputy since 1997. Additional training includes courses at the IMF and the Swiss National Bank.

Bank of Botswana

Linah Mohohlo has been the Governor of the bank since 1999, following a long-term career with the bank in many operational and policy areas. Mohohlo has also served as a Governor for the International Monetary Fund for Botswana. Educational degrees for the governor include a BA in Economics from George Washington University and a MA in Finance and Investments from the University of Exeter, United Kingdom. She has also received executive management training from Yale University.

Central Bank of Cyprus

Chrystalla Georghadji became Governor of the Central Bank of Cyprus and member of the Governing Council of the European Central Bank in 2014. She previously served as Auditor General of the Republic for Cyprus. Educated across the globe, Georghadji holds and an undergraduate degree in economics from the University of Athens, Greece, did postgraduate work in Economics and Econometrics, University of Southampton, UK, and a Master's Degree, University of Chicago.

Central Bank of Honduras

María Elena Mondragón became President of the bank in 2010. She obtained an undergraduate degree in economics at the National University Autonoma de Honduras and a master's degree in economics from Memphis State University. Mondragón has long-term experience as a central banker, previously serving as President of the bank from 2002-2006, along with holding numerous positions at the institution including in the Department of Economics.

Bank of Israel

Karnit Flug was appointed Governor of the bank in 2013, previously serving as Deputy Governor. Flug received her master's degree in Economics from the Hebrew University and her Ph.D. in Economics from Columbia University. She has a strong research background working as an economist at the IMF, Inter-American Development Bank, and the Bank of Israel.

Central Bank of Lesotho

Retselisitsoe Matlanyane was appointed Executive Director and Governor in 2012, serving as Deputy Governor since 2006. She was a lecturer at the National University of Lesotho, prior to joining the central bank. Matlanyane earned a bachelor's degree in economics from the National University of Lesotho, a master's degree in economics from the University of Botswana, and a Ph.D. in economics from the University of Pretoria, South Africa.

Bank Negara Malaysia

Zeti Akhtar Aziz has been Governor and Chairperson since 2000. She holds an undergraduate degree in economics from the University of Malaya and a Ph.D. in monetary and international economics from The Wharton School of the University of Pennsylvania. In 2015, The Wharton School awarded Dr. Aziz the prestigious Dean's Medal for her tremendous impact on the Asia region and beyond, managing the economy during the Asian Financial Crisis of the late 1990s and recently in the global financial downturn.

Maldives Monetary Authority

Azeema Adam was appointed Governor in 2014. Adam has worked at the Maldives Monetary Authority since 1991, holding positions including assistant governor and chief economist. She has a master's in International Development and Finance from the University of Leicester in the UK and a Ph.D. from the University in Canberra, Australia.

Bank of Russia

Elvira Nabiullina became Governor in 2013, having previously served as Russian President Vladimir Putin's economic adviser.

Nabiullina has served as minister of economic development and trade. She holds an undergraduate degree in Science from Moscow State University. Forbes ranked Nabiullina number 71 on the list of the world's most powerful women in 2015 (number 72 in 2014).

Central Bank of Samoa

Atalina Ainuu Enari, economist and lawyer, has been Governor of the bank since 2012. Enari joined the institution in 1991 and has held a variety of positions including senior economist in the international department. The degrees she holds include an undergraduate degree in Business from University of Southern Queensland, Australia, a Master's in International Economics, Banking and Finance from the University of Wales and a Bachelor of Law and Professional Diploma in Legal Practice from the University of the South Pacific.

Central Bank of Sao Tome and Principe

Maria do Carmo Silveira became Governor of the bank for the second time in 2011, previously serving in the role from 1999 to 2005. In the interim Silveria was the prime minister and finance minister from 2005 to 2006. She holds an economics degree from the University of Ukraine.

National Bank of Serbia

Jorgovanka Tabaković became Governor of the bank in 2010. Since 1999 until her appointment as Governor, she worked at a telecommunications company, eventually working as an expert for economic operations. Tabaković holds master's and Ph.D.degrees in economics from the University of Priština, and has experience teaching high school economics.

Central Bank of Seychelles

Caroline Abel has been Governor since 2012, and was formerly the First Deputy Governor. Abel's long-term career with the bank started in 1994 as a bank clerk, assuming many positions over the years. An economist, Abel holds an undergraduate in economics from University of Leeds, UK, and master's degree in monetary economics from University of Glasgow.

National Bank of the Ukraine

Valeriia Gontareva was appointed Governor of the bank in 2013. Gontareva brings a strong banking and financial background to the bank. Her undergraduate degree is from the Kyiv Polytechnic Institute and master's degree from Kyiv National Economic University. Prior to joining the bank, Gontareva was Chairperson for Investment Capital Ukraine.

The Federal Reserve

Janet Yellen was appointed Chair of the Board of Governors of the Federal Reserve System in 2014, serving as Vice Chair prior to the appointment. Yellen had a long-term teaching career and is Professor Emeritus at the University of California at Berkeley. She hold an undergraduate degree in economics from Brown University and a Ph.D. in economics from Yale University. In 2015, Forbes ranked Yellen the fourth he most powerful women in the world. (Yellen was number two in 2014).

Appendix 3

Terms

Asymmetric Information—One party knows more than the other party.
Board of Governors—Main governing body of the Federal Reserve System.
Bond Buying—Large-scale asset purchases by the Federal Reserve of government or government sponsored bonds. The reduced supply of bonds leads to an increase in price and a lowering of interest rates.
Central Bank -- The primary monetary authority of a country. Typically, a nation's central bank issues currency, regulates credit, and oversees the banking system.
Central Banker—A person involved in the high-level executive decisions of the nation's monetary authority. The top position in a central bank is usually referred to as Governor, or occasionally President.
Discount Rate—Interest rate that the Federal Reserve charges a bank to borrow.
Dove—Someone who believes inflation will have minimal negative impact.
Economics—Study of goods and services; the study of the production, distribution, and consumption of goods and services.
Economy—The activities related to the production, distribution, and consumption of goods and services.
Federal Funds—Overnight borrowings between banks.
Federal Reserve System—The central banking system of the U.S.
Financial Institution—Organization offering financial services like savings accounts and investments; examples include banks and brokerage firms.
FOMC—Federal Open Market Committee; makes key decisions about interest rates.
Growth—Steady growth in the productive capacity of the economy.

Hawk—Someone who is concerned about inflation.
IMF –International Monetary Fund. Formed in 1945, an organization of 188 countries seeking stability of the international monetary system.
Inflation—A sustained increase in the general price level of goods and services.
Interest Rate—The percentage rate charged for the use of money.
Keynesian—An economic theory founded by John Maynard Keynes (1883–1946) that government must spend to stimulate the economy during times of a downturn.
M1—Currency, checks, and travelers checks.
M2—M2 includes everything in M1 (currency, checks, and travelers checks) plus savings deposits, small time deposits, and money market mutual funds.
Macroeconomy—The entire economy. Typically, means a country's economy.
Money Supply—The monetary assets in an economy. There are different ways to measure the money supply, common U.S. measurements include M1 and M2.
Nobel Prize—Based on the will of Alfred Nobel, awarded to people, and some organizations, for outstanding research, contributions to society, or inventions.
Reserve Requirements—Amount of funds that a bank must have on hand each night.
Unemployment—People are out of work and actively seeking a job.

Sources

Cussen, Mark P. "Janet Yellen: Background and Philosophy." *www.Investopedia.com*. October 16, 2013. Retrieved August 6, 2014.

"Fort Hamilton grad Janet Yellen is first woman nominated to chair the Federal Reserve." *www.Homereporternews.com*. October 9, 2013. Retrieved August 6, 2014.

Howard, Caroline. (Ed.) "The World's 100 Most Powerful Women." March 26, 2015. www.forbes.com. Retrieved August 11, 2015.

"Janet Yellen." Board of Governors of the Federal Reserve System. *www.Federalreservesystem.gov*. February 3, 2014. Retrieved August 7, 2014.

Kolhatkar, Sheelah and Matthew Philips. "Who is Janet Yellen? A Look at the Front-Runner for the Next Fed Chairman." *www.Businessweek.com*. September 19, 2013. Retrieved August 6, 2014.

Reedy, Sudeep and Rebecca Ballhaus. "Janet Yellen's Short and Storied Newspaper Career." *Real Time Economics, The Wall Street Journal. www.blogs.wsj.com*. October 9, 2013. Retrieved August 6, 2014.

Sang, Amie. "Women of the World's Central Banks." *The World*. http://blogs.ft.com/the-world/. October 3, 2013. Retrieved August 11, 2015.

"Vice Chair Janet L. Yellen: Confirmation hearing before the Committee on Banking, Housing, and Urban Affairs, U.S. Senate, Washington, DC, November 14, 2013. *www.Federalreservesystem.gov*. Retrieved August 9, 2014.

Yellen, Janet. "A Painfully Slow Recovery for America's Workers: Causes, Implications, and the Federal Reserve's Response." Presented at the A Trans-Atlantic Agenda for Shared Prosperity conference sponsored by the AFL-CIO, Friedrich Ebert Stiftung, and the IMK Macroeconomic Policy Institute, Washington, DC, February 11, 2013. *www.Federalreservesystem.gov*. Retrieved August 10, 2014.

OTHER ANAPHORA LITERARY PRESS TITLES

Film Theory and Modern Art
Editor: Anna Faktorovich

Interview with Larry Niven
Editor: Anna Faktorovich

Dragonflies in the Cowburbs
Donelle Dreese

Domestic Subversive
Roberta Salper

Radical Agrarian Economics
Anna Faktorovich

Fajitas and Beer Convention
Roger Rodriguez

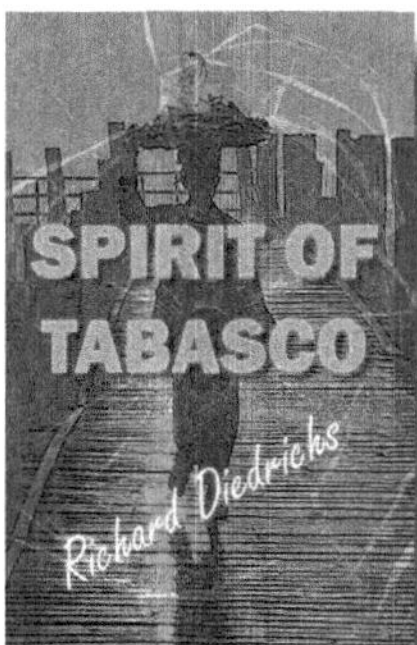

Spirit of Tabasco
Richard Diedrichs

Skating in Concord
Jean LeBlanc

Printed by BoD™in Norderstedt, Germany

9 781681 142036